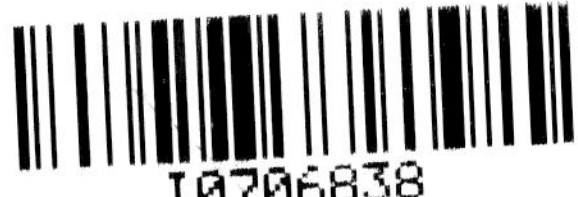

THIS BOOK BELONGS TO

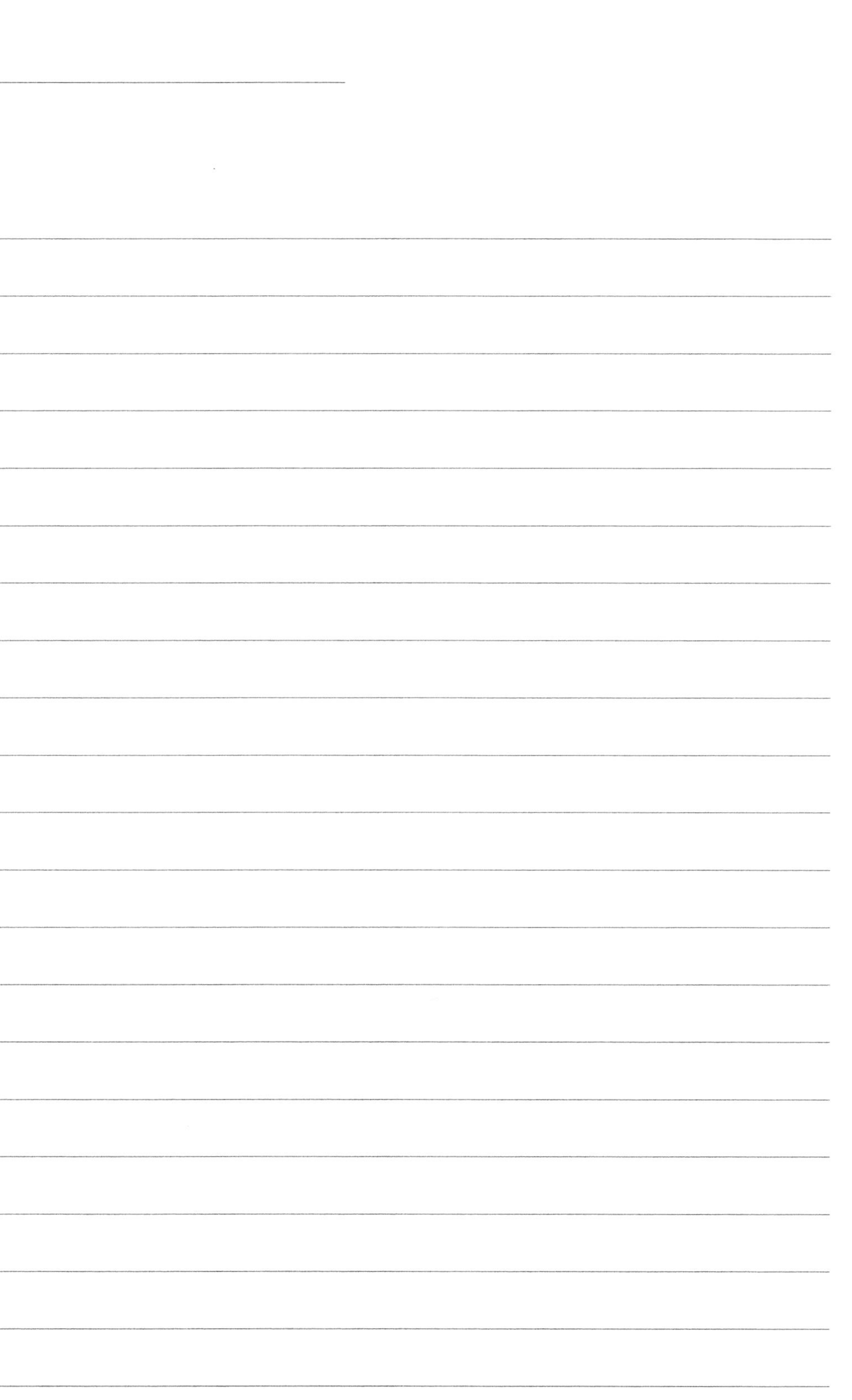

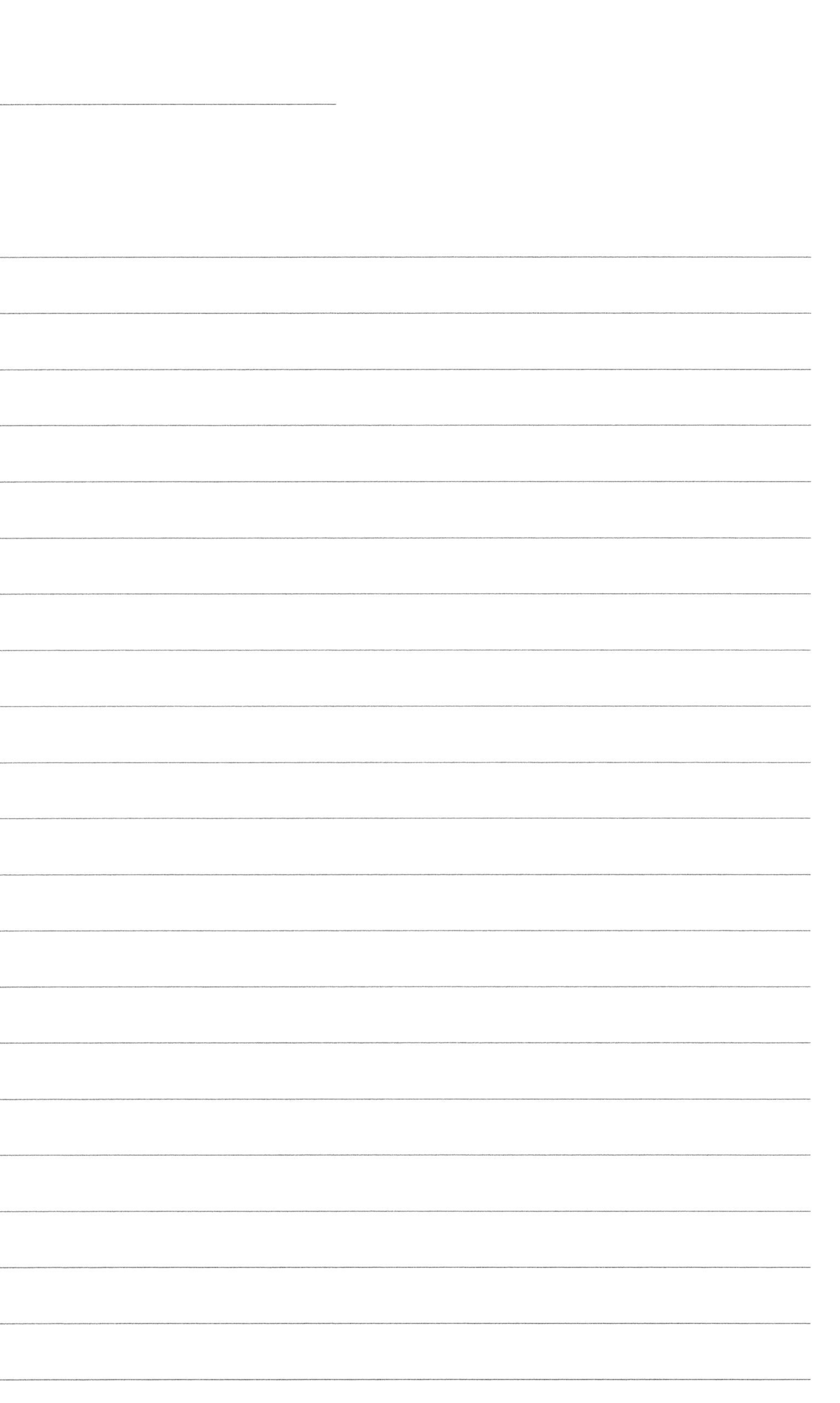

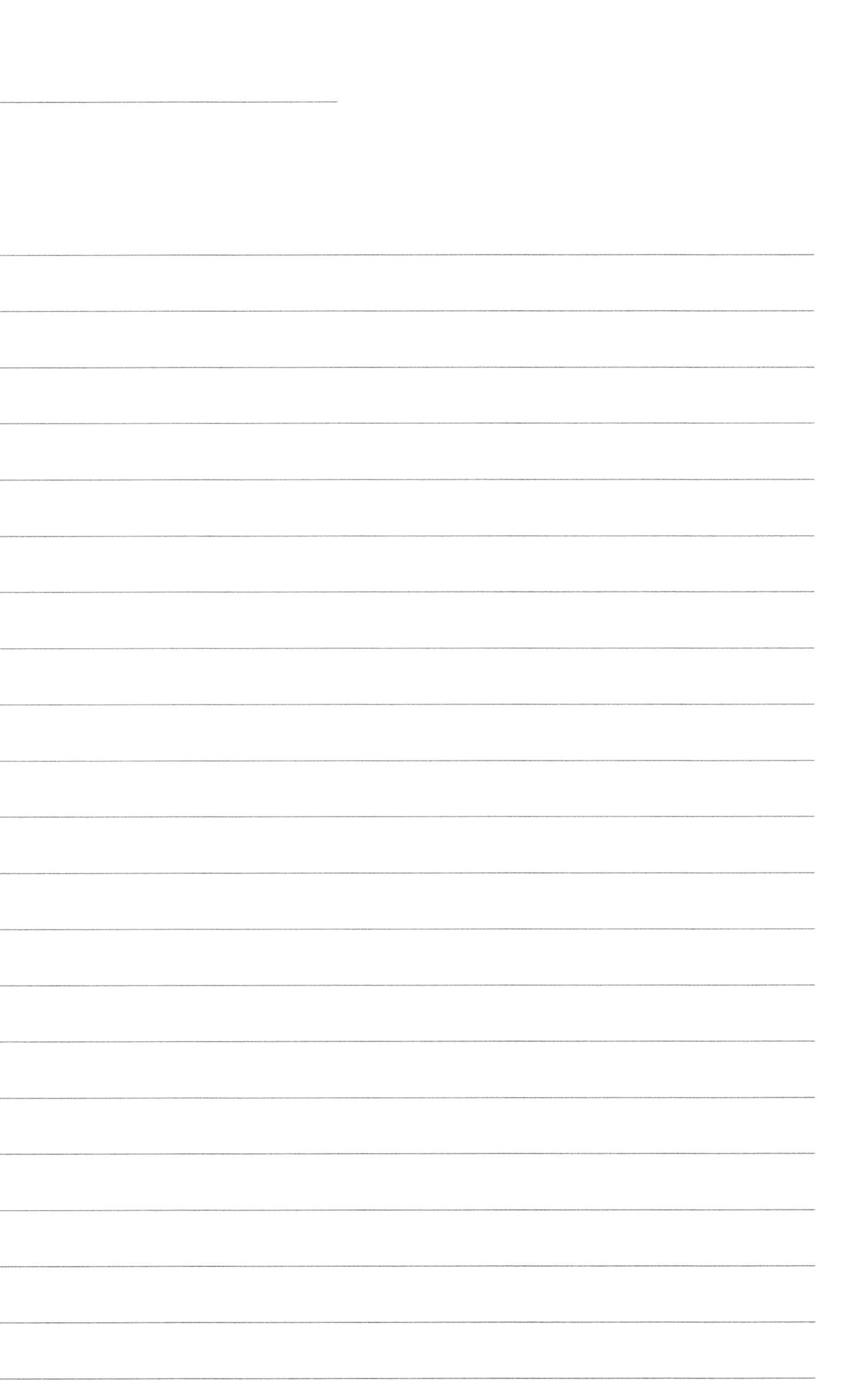

www.ingramcontent.com/pod-product-compliance
Lightning Source LLC
Chambersburg PA
CBHW070900250726
48662CB00003B/1481

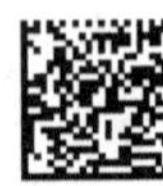

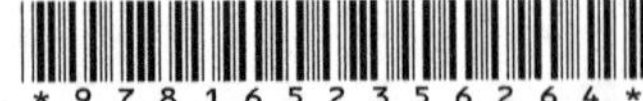